OBSOLETE

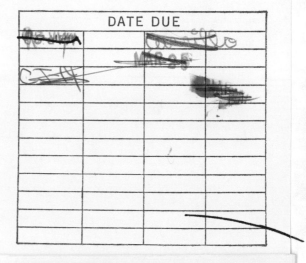

Women and Science

Cover by Jackie Denison

Illustrations by Jane Palecek

Library of Congress Number: 79-13659

1   2   3   4   5   6   7   8   9   0   83   82   81   80   79

Printed and bound in the United States of America.

Library of Congress Cataloging in Publication Data
McLenighan, Valjean.
  Women and science.

  Bibliography: p. 48
  SUMMARY: Presents brief career biographies of
women prominent in the field of science, including
Florence Sabin, Chien Shiung Wu, Margaret Mead, and
Alice Hamilton.
    1. Women in science—Juvenile literature.
[1. Women scientists. 2. Scientists] I. Palecek,
Jane. II. Title.
Q130.M32   509'.2'2 [B] [920]   79-13659
ISBN O-8172-1379-1 lib. bdg.

WOMEN
AND SCIENCE

Valjean McLenighan

RAINTREE PUBLISHERS
Milwaukee • Toronto • Melbourne • London

CONTENTS

INTRODUCTION

Today, there are more opportunities for American women in science than ever before. But the number of women scientists is still small.

There have always been more men in American science than women. In the past, girls were not encouraged, as much as boys were, to take an interest in science as a career.

Also, many years ago, women did not have the same chances for an education that men did. Elizabeth Blackwell, America's first woman doctor, was turned down by twenty-nine medical schools before she was admitted — as a joke — to New York's Geneva College in 1847. She graduated as the top student in her class and even then was not allowed to practice medicine in New York hospitals.

Women have continued, however, to challenge the belief that science is a man's field — and they have proved it false. Women who have chosen science as a career have made outstanding contributions in the field. This book provides a look at six women and their careers in science.

ANNIE JUMP CANNON

It [a star's spectrum] is not just a streak of light to me, but a gateway to a wonderful new world.

Annie Jump Cannon

How patient are you? On the next clear night, step outside, and if you're lucky, you may see as many as one or two thousand stars.

What if you wanted to make a catalog, or list, of every star you could see? Would you give each star a name? Or would you give them numbers? In what order would you put them? How long do you think it would take you to make the list?

For Annie Jump Cannon, it took all her working life. As the world's leading woman astronomer, she cataloged more than 300,000 stars in her

6

lifetime. Though she died in 1941, her work is still the standard that astronomers — scientists who study the sky — use today. Besides working out a system to cover almost every kind of star known to science, Annie Jump Cannon made a few discoveries of her own. In fact, she was the first astronomer to spot more than 300 new stars.

Annie was born on December 11, 1863. She was the only daughter, and the oldest of the three children, of Wilson Lee Cannon and Mary Elizabeth (Jump) Cannon. As a child in Dover, Delaware, Annie loved to be up high. Her favorite spot in the big white house where she grew up was the attic. It had a trap door that led to the roof, where Annie often climbed to stargaze. By candlelight, she would spend hours in the attic, going over her mother's old astronomy books. Annie was always very close to her mother. Early in life, the little girl learned to share her mother's interest in the stars.

Another thing she loved to do was gaze at rainbows. A candleholder in the living room was hung with tinkling crystals. When light shone through them, they made lovely rainbows on the wall and ceiling. Annie could look at them for hours.

Annie expected to grow up to be a society lady in Dover. She was a pretty girl and she had lots of friends. But her teachers found in her a special quickness of mind, and they urged her father to send her to college.

Mr. Cannon chose Wellesley College in Massachusetts, which had opened its doors five years

Annie Jump Cannon

before. Annie studied with Professor Sarah F. Whiting, a great teacher of physics and astronomy. Years later, Annie still remembered what fun it had been to troop outdoors, night after night, with Miss Whiting's astronomy class to view the Great Comet of 1882.

Though the only real equipment they had was a four-inch telescope, Miss Whiting saw to it that her class knew about all the latest developments in astronomy. One of these was star spectroscopy — a way of learning about stars by studying the rainbow patters they made when photographed through a prism.

Annie had a wonderful time in college, and she did very well. But when she graduated, in 1884,

8

Annie Jump Cannon is shown examining a star chart.

she returned to Dover with no other thought than to take up the life she had always expected to lead.

For ten years Annie lived the carefree life of a beautiful society woman of Dover. But when her mother died suddenly, Annie went into shock. Reading no longer interested her; her friends were very kind, but they couldn't ease her deep sense of loss. In her grief, she turned to the skies. Their vastness and beauty comforted her. The questions they raised, which she had puzzled over as a child and studied at Wellesley, returned to grip and hold her mind.

In 1894, Annie went back to Wellesley to study with Professor Whiting. Soon she was taking an astronomy course at nearby Radcliffe College. Early

9

in 1896 she went to work as an assistant at the Harvard University Observatory, one of the best places in the world to study the stars.

Her job was to classify stars according to their spectra — the ribbons of color they made when photographed through a prism. By studying a star's color, scientists can tell its temperature, size, age, and how fast it is spinning through space. At that time, Harvard had the world's largest collection of star photographs. But a workable system of putting the pictures in order had never been found.

Annie arranged and rearranged the system then in use until it was just about perfect. She identified several main classes of stars and divided each one into sub-classes, using letters and numbers to name them. Annie's system was so simple, yet flexible, that it was later adopted by the International Astronomical Union. Astronomers still use this system today.

Annie loved working with spectra — the same rainbows that had charmed her as a child. "It is not just a streak of light," she said, "but a gateway to a wonderful new world." She had a natural talent for identifying stars — her mind held perfect pictures, not just of the main types of stars, but also of the smallest sub-classes. As the months and years went by, she learned to classify star spectra faster and more accurately than anyone else in the world.

In 1911, Dr. Edward C. Pickering, director of the Harvard Observatory, put Annie in charge of the entire collection of photographs. She was curator of astronomical photographs until 1938, when she was appointed to the Harvard University faculty.

Her work between 1911 and 1924 has been described as "amazing." She began by classifying 5,000 stars a month, and her output grew with the years. The result was Harvard's *Henry Draper Catalogue,* nine volumes listing all the stars between the North and South Poles of the sky — more than a quarter-million stars.

Annie did not work to achieve fame or because she had nothing else to do. She worked because she truly enjoyed it. After a day spent studying photographs, she often would climb to the observatory telescope and gaze at the night sky. She discovered some 300 new variable stars — stars that grow bright, then dim, then bright again. She also found five new novae, or exploding stars.

Many honors came to her during her lifetime. Annie Jump Cannon was the first woman to receive honorary degrees from Oxford University in England, and the University of Groningen in the Netherlands. The Royal Astronomical Society named her one of its few honorary members; the National Academy of Sciences gave her a medal for her achievements.

She also set up an award — the Annie Jump Cannon Prize — to recognize outstanding women astronomers. Though there have been many fine women in her profession, Annie Jump Cannon remains famous as the woman who identified and classified more stars then anyone else in the world.

RACHEL CARSON

I had said I could never again listen happily to a thrush song if I had not done all I could.

Rachel Carson

In June 1963, a woman author sat before a special U.S. Senate committee on pollution control. She was largely responsible for the creation of the committee. Calmly and expertly, fifty-five-year old Rachel Carson answered the senators' questions about pesticides — poisonous chemicals used to kill insect pests in the United States.

Today, *pollution* is a word that most people understand. But twenty years ago, very few people knew what the word meant because few people were concerned about pollution. Rachel Carson's book *Silent Spring* was a strong warning against the dangers of pesticides. Published in 1962, the book shocked many Americans into taking a long, hard look at the way they were treating planet earth.

Rachel Carson was born on May 27, 1907. The daughter of Robert Warden Carson and Maria McLean Carson, she grew up in Springdale, Pennsylvania, not far from Pittsburgh. On her family's farm, Rachel developed a sense of wonder at the beauty and mystery of nature. She also had a way with words. By the time she reached the fourth grade, Rachel knew she wanted to be a writer.

Always a top student, Rachel graduated from high school in 1925 and wanted to go to college. Though money was scarce, Mrs. Carson was determined that her daughter would have a chance to be whatever she wanted. She saved as much money as she could to help Rachel pay her college tuition. Scholarship money and loans helped Rachel with the rest of the expenses.

At the Pennsylvania College for Women, today known as Chatham College, Rachel wrote prize-winning stories for the college newspaper and magazine. After taking a biology course, however, Rachel's interest in nature and science was reawakened. She continued with her writing, but changed her major from English to biology — the study of living things. She graduated with honors in 1929.

Three years later, she received her Master's Degree from Johns Hopkins University. Rachel's

13

training as a marine biologist — a scientist who studies the oceans and ocean creatures — was complete. Years later she said, "Ever since childhood, I've been fascinated by the sea, and my mind has stored up everything I have ever learned about it."

As a marine biologist, Rachel found it hard to find a job in her field. During the next three years she taught at Johns Hopkins and the University of Maryland. She also did some work in a marine biological laboratory in Massachusetts.

When her father died in 1935, Rachel was faced with the responsibility of caring for her mother. She went to work — on a part-time, temporary basis — for the U.S. Bureau of Fisheries. She was paid a salary of $19.25 a week. Her job was to write a series of radio scripts about fishing and sea life. These "Seven-Minute Fish Stories" were so popular that the bureau asked her to turn them into a booklet. So, in 1936, Rachel became a full-time employee earning $38.48 a week. Her new job gave her a chance to use her knowledge as a biologist and as a writer.

Besides taking care of her mother, Rachel was also supporting two nieces and she needed extra money. She sometimes sold articles to magazines and newspapers to add to her income. One day, Rachel sent an essay she had written to the *Atlantic Monthly*, a leading literary magazine. Six weeks later the magazine mailed her a check for $75 and told Rachel her essay would appear in the September 1937 issue.

The essay Rachel had written was titled "Undersea." Critics described it as "beautifully written" and said that it was an unusual blend of good scientific knowledge and good writing. The article was really an introduction to marine ecology — the study of the sea's living creatures in relation to their surroundings and each other. An editor for a publishing firm liked Rachel's article and asked her to consider writing a book on the same subject as the magazine article.

The book took four years to finish. *Under the Sea Wind* was published at the end of 1941. The critics praised it, but the book was lost in the uproar over America's entrance into World War II. People had other things on their minds than ocean life, and *Under the Sea Wind* sold only 5,000 copies.

Meanwhile, Rachel worked steadily at her government job. By 1948, she was head of the Information Division of the U.S. Fish and Wildlife Service. She planned a series of a dozen booklets on wildlife conservation. But there was no place in the Information Division for the book she really wanted to write about oceanography — the total study of the sea.

The Sea Around Us was published in July, 1951. Rachel's book about oceanography stayed on the bestseller lists for the next year and a half. Newspaper editors named Rachel "Woman of the Year in Literature," and she won the National Book Award.

For the first time in her adult life, Rachel didn't

Rachel Carson is shown here in 1963. She was in Washington, D.C., testifying before a government committee that was studying the use of pesticides.

have to worry about money. In 1952, she left her job at the Fish and Wildlife Service and started to write full-time. Her third book, *The Edge of the Sea*, came out in 1955. It also was a success.

In January, 1958, Rachel received a letter from a friend, describing what had happened when a plane sprayed her property with DDT, an insecticide used to kill mosquitoes. Seven songbirds had died at once, followed by three more the next morning. "I emptied and scrubbed the birdbath after the spraying," Rachel's friend wrote, "but you can never kill DDT."

Rachel had found the subject of her next book. The use of DDT and other pesticides had grown quickly in the 1940s. Billions of pounds of the chemical had been spread across hundreds of thousands of square miles of American farmland, towns, and forests.

As early as 1946, scientists had begun to worry about the effect of pesticides on living creatures. The chemicals were strong poisons. A very tiny dose was enough to harm or even kill wildlife. By 1958, the U.S. Congress had begun studying the effects of pesticides on wildlife. The alarm had been sounded in official circles, but the public knew very little about DDT or chemicals like it.

People didn't know that almost all of their food showed traces of the chemicals. They didn't know that DDT doesn't wash off and doesn't disappear in cooking. The public didn't know that dangerous poisons were building up in the soil and washing into rivers and streams — polluting their drinking water. There was almost no place on earth that was completely free of pesticide pollution.

In 1958, no one knew what amount of DDT would harm a human being, but scientists were studying its effects on animals. They knew DDT had killed many fish and birds and had caused sickness in other animals.

Rachel spent a year gathering and studying material. The more she learned, the more she wanted to tell people, as clearly and powerfully as she could, about the dangers of pesticides. She did not suggest that all pesticides be banned forever.

But she did believe that there were other, safer ways of controlling troublesome insects.

Her book, *Silent Spring*, caused a sensation when it was published in 1962. First-year sales topped 250,000 copies. The book was discussed in newspapers and magazines all over the country. People wrote letters expressing their concern about pesticides to the Congress and other government agencies. President Kennedy formed a special government group to study pesticides.

The chemical industry — the producers of the pesticides — struck back with a campaign to protect its image. Articles began to appear which told the public how lucky it was to have chemical pesticides. DDT and chemicals like it were presented as the only practical defense against insects that could cause mass starvation and disease. Some of the articles quoted statements that Rachel had never made. There were personal attacks on Rachel, too. Stories were printed that made her seem foolish. Some people suggested that she was a crackpot. One reader wrote the *New Yorker* magazine: "Miss Carson is obviously a Communist. She is opposed to American business. We can live without birds but not without business."

An hour-long television special in April 1963, gave *Silent Spring* an even wider audience. The president's Science Advisory Committee reported to the Senate in May, confirming the dangers that Rachel had warned against. The news was broadcast in the special television report.

Rachel was given many honors. She became the

first woman to receive the National Audubon Society Medal, and she was elected to the American Academy of Arts and Letters. She also won awards from the American Geographical Society and the National Council of Women.

When Rachel Carson completed *Silent Spring* it is said that she went into her study, turned on a Beethoven violin concerto and wept. Her words were, "I had said I could never again listen happily to a thrush song if I had not done all I could. And the thoughts of all the birds and other creatures and all the loveliness that is in nature came to me with such a surge of happiness, now that I had done what I could."

Rachel Carson died — April 14, 1964 — less than two years after her book was published. On December 31, 1972, the U.S. Government enacted laws to ban the use of DDT and some other chemical pesticides in the United States.

ALICE HAMILTON

I chose it [medicine] because as a doctor I could go anywhere I pleased — to far-off lands or to city slums — and be quite sure that I could be of use . . .

Alice Hamilton

In the early 1900s, Alice Hamilton had to be part detective and part doctor to prove that workers were being poisoned in factories where chemicals, such as lead, were used. Her job was to report on occupational disease — illness caused by unsafe and unhealthy working conditions — in the state of Illinois.

Many of the plants and factories that Dr. Hamilton visited had nice, new modern machinery, but they also had air that was filled with lead dust and fumes. These were poisons. Workers who breathed these fumes all day often became ill. Many of the workers had just moved to America, and didn't even speak English. They didn't report their illness because they were afraid of losing their jobs.

Alice talked to the managers of each of the plants. She tried to convince them to change certain things to make the working conditions safe. But the owners and managers wanted proof that there really was a problem. And, this was when Alice had to play detective as well as doctor.

She would hear that a worker named "Joe" was out sick with "lead." Then Alice might have to talk with five or six people before discovering "Joe's" last name and where he lived. In the early 1900s, workers were paid in cash, rather than by payroll check. Companies did not keep employee records with information such as addresses.

After learning "Joe's" full name and "about" where he lived, Dr. Hamilton would search for his home. If she was lucky, she would talk with the worker who was ill.

After Dr. Hamilton talked with a worker who had lead poisoning, she would then have to find his hospital records to prove the cause of illness to the owner of the plant where the man worked. She was very familiar with the many forms that lead poisoning could take — from loss of weight and weakness to shaking, paralysis, coma, mental breakdown, and even death. In 1910, however, most doctors did not know about the signs of lead poisoning.

Dr. Hamilton visited many plants during her

year as head of the Illinois Occupational Disease Commission. She studied the lead industry, while other members of her team investigated diseases associated with the brass trades, coal mines, steel mills, and other industries. Although industrial medicine was well advanced in Europe, diseases of American industry had never been studied.

Workers and factory owners alike were not aware that it was very dangerous to work with certain materials in unsafe conditions. In 1910, occupational disease was widespread in America. Almost one-half of the workers in one factory which Dr. Hamilton visited developed lead poisoning in a period of six months. Once factory owners knew how, many were eager to improve the working conditions. Alice provided suggestions to help them. However, nothing could be done about those who refused to make changes. There were no laws to regulate safety standards or to help diseased workers.

The situation changed in 1911. The Illinois Occupational Disease Commission's report led to America's first workmen's compensation law, which was passed by the Illinois legislature. The law stated that workers who became ill or were injured because of their jobs had the right to receive benefits.

The Illinois commission's work was completed. But Dr. Hamilton's was just beginning. At the age of forty, she had finally found her true lifework. Almost single-handedly, she founded the field of American industrial medicine.

Born on February 27, 1869, Alice Hamilton grew

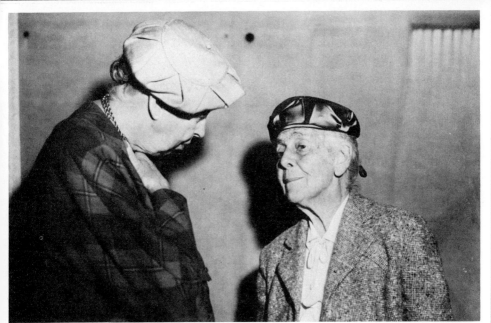

Alice Hamilton (right) is shown with Eleanor Roosevelt.

up in Fort Wayne, Indiana. Her family was well-to-do and educated. As a teenager, Alice decided she wanted to be a doctor.

She earned her medical degree at the University of Michigan and went to work in an immigrant neighborhood in Boston. Many of her patients were poor. She loved them and learned to understand their problems. Her work in Boston fulfilled a personal need — to serve her fellow humans.

However, Alice found one part of her work very difficult. If one of her patients died, she felt great pain and grief. She worried that her emotional attitude weakened her as a doctor. So she decided to become a laboratory researcher.

For the next twelve years, she taught and also conducted research. During this time, she lived in Chicago, Illinois, at Hull House — the settlement founded by Jane Addams to serve the great number

23

of immigrant poor who came from Europe to America at the beginning of the century. During her free time, Dr. Hamilton started a clinic for children in the basement of Hull House. She also taught adult education classes.

Alice's work as a teacher and researcher fulfilled her need to use her mind. Living at Hull House gave her the chance to serve others. Still, her life was not complete.

This was the point when Governor Deneen of Illinois asked Dr. Hamilton to head up a team to study industrial sickness in the state. Dr. Hamilton enjoyed the work so much that she never returned to the laboratory.

In 1911, Alice was hired by the Federal Department of Labor to study occupational disease in the United States. Her work in Illinois had only scratched the surface. She began to investigate the lead trades, and other industries as well.

When World War I began, she turned her attention to the thousands of workers in munitions plants where ammunition and explosives were made. At that time, little was known about how the new gases, acids, and chemicals would affect human beings.

Because of her work, Alice often placed herself in dangerous situations. She was exposed daily to industrial working conditions in many different plants. If the workers were not protected from poisonous fumes she wasn't either. In one plant, eight vats of acid exploded, and she fled outdoors with the workers to escape the huge, rolling orange clouds of poison gas.

She worked hard, but her reports were too late to help many workers during World War I. By the time of World War II, however, most of the dangers of the military chemical industry had been reduced or eliminated. The U.S. Government opened a special office to handle cases involving industrial poisoning. And, by this time, most of the states where industries existed had passed laws about job safety and benefits for workers with occupational diseases.

Industrial medicine had arrived. Harvard University created a new department to train doctors in the young and growing field. Dr. Alice Hamilton was the best qualified person in the country to head the new department. She was the first woman ever asked to serve on the Harvard faculty.

The department devoted to the study of industrial medicine started with a very small number of students, but it grew quickly.

At the age of sixty-seven, Dr. Hamilton retired from Harvard University. But she continued to work as an advisor to industry and government.

Born shortly after the Civil War, Alice Hamilton lived to be 101 years old — long enough to see the dawn of the nuclear age. During an interview when she was ninety, she warned that "new industries, new materials, new processes often create new dangers." She was especially concerned about how atomic waste material would be stored and disposed of.

"I worry about it," she said, "But I keep hoping. Maybe tomorrow or the next day will bring a solution."

MARGARET MEAD

Knowledge joined to action — knowledge about what man has been and is — can protect the future.

Margaret Mead

She was called a "busybody" and a "goody-goody," as well as a genius. She was criticized for acting like a man and also for being too much of a lady. Although popular opinion of Margaret Mead varied, she was one of the world's most famous social scientists. Even her critics admit that her ideas have "been felt in almost every leader of American thought."

Born December 16, 1901, Margaret was raised in and around Philadelphia, Pennsylvania. She was known in the family as the "Original Punk" — the first child of Emily and Edward Mead.

Her father, a university professor of economics, taught her that the only thing worth doing in life was "adding to the store of the world's exact knowledge." Margaret's mother was a social scientist — a person who studies human societies.

Since the family lived in many different places while she was growing up, Margaret didn't spend much time in grammar school. Her mother and grandmother taught her at home.

Margaret's childhood experiences helped her with her later work as an anthropologist — a social scientist who studies the arts, beliefs, and customs of different groups of people.

When Margaret was ten, her mother taught her to keep detailed notes on the actions of her two younger sisters — in the same way that a social scientist would. Margaret learned to pay attention to other people and to record their actions quickly and accurately. She tried to find patterns in how her little sisters behaved. She wondered about the ways they were alike and the ways they were different from each other.

At Barnard College in New York, twenty-one year old Margaret became friends with two famous anthropologists, Franz Boas and Ruth Benedict. Anthropology was a new, exciting subject. Anthropologists called fieldworkers visited different places and studied societies of people by living among them and learning their ways of doing things.

Margaret Mead (right) is shown in 1953 with a mother and child of the Admiralty Islands.

When anthropologists studied these tribes of people, they looked at how the tribe provided food, clothing, and shelter; how families were organized; how rules were made, and what the language and ceremonies of the tribe were.

The fieldworker's goal in each study was to find out what was the same in the various cultures and what was different. And, the long-range goal of anthropology was to reach a better understanding of human nature by studying how different groups of people lived.

Margaret graduated from Barnard College in 1923. As a graduate student at Columbia University, she decided she wanted to study societies of people in the South Pacific islands. On her first field trip, in 1925 and 1926, she spent nine months among the people of Samoa, an island in the South Pacific.

During this time, she learned the Samoan language and got used to eating raw fish and sleeping on pebble floors. She lived the life of the Samoan girls and women. Margaret fished with them and helped them weave and cook. She filled notebook after notebook with her observations of the people and their customs.

When Margaret returned to America, she put her findings in a book, *Coming of Age in Samoa*, which was published in 1928. A common idea about "human nature" at that time was that the teenage years were always difficult. "It's human nature," many people said, "for teenagers to be sulky, high-strung, and rebellious. Their bodies are changing, they're becoming adults — it's all part of the painful process of growing up."

In fact, Margaret pointed out in her book, growing up in Samoa wasn't at all painful for the girls she had lived with. In the Samoan culture, the passage from childhood into the adult world seemed to be a smooth one. Margaret's studies suggested that the "difficult teenage years" were not a result of "human nature." If it were "natural" for the teenage years to be difficult, then the Samoan teenagers would have had the same experience.

During the next eleven years, she made several visits to the South Pacific to study different groups of people living there. She learned seven languages and found new ways to record information about the various cultures she studied. She saw that human nature could be vastly different from one culture to the next.

In one tribe, women took care of business matters while the men stayed home. In another tribe, the roles were switched. For a while, Margaret lived among a group of people who argued and fought all the time. Then she studied a tribe of people who went to sleep instead of fighting.

This wide range of experiences stretched Margaret's ideas and raised many questions about human nature. Are people's personalities naturally different from the time they are born? Do both males and females share certain basic personality traits? Margaret shared her findings and thoughts on these and many other questions in a number of books.

In 1939, Margaret and her husband Gregory Bateson, who was also an anthropologist, had a child — Mary Catherine Bateson. World War II kept Margaret from doing any fieldwork, so she turned her attention to other societies, such as the United States. She wrote, served on research committees, and gave lectures about the things she had learned from past fieldwork.

Based on her observations of other cultures, Margaret challenged traditional opinions about human nature. For example, many people believed that war and violence were simply a part of life, and that it was impossible for them not to exist. But Margaret had observed societies where people

Margaret Mead is pictured at an art gallery in 1966.
Behind her is a photograph from a book she had written
about family life around the world.

31

lived and worked together peacefully, without war or fighting.

Also, most people in America at that time thought that it was against "human nature" for women to work outside the home. Margaret, however, had studied societies where it was "natural" for the women to work while the men stayed home to take care of the children and domestic chores.

In the 1950s, Margaret revisited the islands where she had done fieldwork twenty years earlier. Since her last visit, modern technology had even found its way to some of the societies in the South Sea islands. Great changes had taken place. People who had never seen a bicycle had stepped "straight from the Stone Age into an airplane," she explained.

The birth of the atomic age marked the beginning of what Margaret, who had become Dr. Mead by this time, saw as a global culture — a greater worldwide sharing of customs, beliefs, and ways of life than ever before in history. She hoped this sharing would lead to new solutions to age-old human problems, such as people from different backgrounds and countries understanding each other as fellow human beings.

World famous anthropologist, Dr. Margaret Mead, was actively involved with her work most of her life. In addition to field trips and writing books, she worked with the World Federation of Mental Health, the World Council of Churches and the United Nations. She also served as head of the Americans Association for the Advancement of Science.

Margaret Mead was associated with the American Museum of Natural History for over fifty years. In 1970, a dream of her's was realized when the museum opened its Hall of the Peoples of the Pacific, containing a record of her lifework.

As controversial as she was hardworking, Margaret Mead spoke her opinions boldly and honestly. She thought that the idea of lifetime marriage was out-of-date. Instead, she suggested two kinds of marriage — one between people who did not want children and one for couples who did.

Dr. Mead was named to the Women's Hall of Fame in 1976 — the same year she celebrated her seventy-fifth birthday. Her interests continued to expand. In 1977, she became the head of a group called New Directions. Its job, she said, was to "get ideas started, spread them fast in different forms, until what seemed impossible . . . yesterday is a shared activity of thousands tomorrow."

At the age of seventy-six, Dr. Margaret Mead was as tireless a worker as when she was twenty-three and made her first trip to Samoa. At a party celebrating her fifty-year anniversary with the American Museum she declared, "Sooner or later I'm going to die. But I'm not going to retire."

The woman who was anthropologist, psychologist, writer, lecturer, teacher — and more — died November 15, 1978. True to her word, Margaret Mead was still contributing to "the store of the world's exact knowledge" in the year of her death.

FLORENCE SABIN

The important thing is the progress of knowledge and not which individual is the relay runner who for a brief span carried the torch.

Florence Sabin

When Colorado Governor John Vivian appointed seventy-four-year-old Florence Sabin to head his subcommittee on health, he had no idea what he was getting into.

This committee was one of several the governor organized when World War II was coming to an end. A woman newspaper reporter warned him that he was "asking for trouble" if he didn't name at least one woman as head of a committee. She suggested he appoint Florence Sabin.

The governor asked his political friends what they thought of Dr. Sabin. Would she cause trouble by having too many ideas and wanting to make changes? Would she want to be paid a lot of money for her work? And what if she didn't do anything at all?

The governor's friends reassured him with comments like "Oh, she won't give you trouble . . . She's a nice old lady with her hair in a bun and a quite friendly smile. You might like her. Everyone does."

Little did the governor know that during the next three years, that "nice old lady" would create a sensation when she began a campaign to clean up Colorado. First, she had to convince people that there was a problem. She would explain that while Colorado lost 2,699 soldiers during World War II, 8,245 Colorado citizens died — in the same amount of time — from diseases that could have been prevented. One person every six hours was dying needlessly for lack of a good public health program.

As a result of her work, Colorado would have one of the best public health programs in the nation. And Florence Sabin would conclude her third successful career. She had already retired as a teacher and a scientist. Her third endeavor in Colorado would earn her the title — humanitarian.

On November 9, 1871, Florence Rena Sabin was born in Central City, Colorado. Her father, George Sabin, was a miner. Florence's mother, Serena Sabin, died when Florence was seven years old. Her death came shortly after the birth of Florence's little brother, Albert.

The two Sabin daughters, Florence and Mary, were sent to Wolfe Hall, a boarding school in Denver. Florence was homesick and cried every night. When her little brother, Albert, died a year later, she lost all interest in lessons, food, and games.

George Sabin worked away from home much of the time, so he sent Florence and Mary to live with an aunt and uncle in Chicago. Florence's Uncle Albert understood her shyness and shared her interest in books. Aunt Min gave Florence motherly affection and care.

When Florence was twelve, she and Mary moved to Vermont Academy. Florence was a good student, and she was elected president of her class in her senior year of high school. By the time she graduated, both her grandparents had died. Florence, faced with the loss of two more people she loved, followed her sister Mary to Smith College.

Florence's shyness of earlier years returned. She studied very hard and earned her best grades in science courses. Once, when she was suposed to be doing her homework, she found herself doodling instead. She wrote *Florence Sabin, M.D.* over and over again. One of Florence's teachers was a doctor. She urged Florence to study medicine, but warned " . . . even today, a woman doctor is a pioneer."

After college graduation in 1893, Florence returned to Wolfe Hall to teach and earn money so that she could go to medical school. At the end of the year at Wolfe Hall, Mrs. Ella Strong Denison, the wife of a wealthy Denver doctor, offered Florence a summer job. The job was teaching science to Mrs. Denison's children and their cousins at the family's cottage in Wisconsin. Florence accepted.

That summer job was the beginning of a friendship with Mrs. Denison and her family that would last a lifetime. Mrs. Denison liked and trusted Florence.

She helped the Denison children learn about nature by letting them explore its beauty and wonder for themselves, rather than just telling them about it. It was a way of teaching that worked for her throughout her career.

Florence returned to Wolfe Hall to teach for another year. The next fall she was the first woman student admitted to the Johns Hopkins University Medical School.

Her work as a medical student was outstanding. By the time Florence graduated in 1900 — the first woman graduate of that medical school — she had completed a detailed study of the brain.

Florence was happier doing research than taking care of patients. After her work on the brain, she turned to the lymphatic system — the vessels that carry the important fluid called lymph to every part of the body. Not much was known about the lymphatic system in 1900. Dr. Sabin's pioneer research on this system was recognized as one of the greatest scientific advancements in decades.

When the head of the John Hopkins anatomy

Florence Sabin is shown at work in her laboratory.
At this time, she was studying blood cells.

department died in 1917, many people assumed that Florence would take over the position. Instead, the university appointed her to a lesser job. Many of her students protested, and some wondered if she would leave after such poor treatment. "I'll stay, of course," she told her concerned students. "I have research to do."

To ease her disappointment, Florence plunged back into her research work — this time studying blood cells. The results of this study, combined with her earlier work, led to a better understanding of how the body fights infection and disease. Florence had added greatly to medicine's store of knowledge, and she was honored accordingly. She was chosen to welcome Marie Curie, the pioneering physicist, to America in 1921. That same year she went to Peking, China, to address the Union Medical College. There she received her first medal. And, among many other honors, she was the first woman ever elected to the American Academy of Science.

Although Florence felt honored by all the attention, she was annoyed at being called a woman scientist. To her thinking, science had no sex. Still, she realized that she was blazing a trail for other women to follow, and she did everything she could to encourage women in all fields to try for excellence.

In 1925, Dr. Sabin left Johns Hopkins to work at the Rockefeller Institute for Medical Research in New York. During the next thirteen years she worked on eleven different studies having to do with blood cells. The research team she selected made important discoveries about tuberculosis and found new ways of studying infections and allergies.

By the time Dr. Florence Sabin retired, in 1938, she had received many more awards and honorary degrees. At the age of sixty-seven, she went back to Denver. But she couldn't sit still for long. Soon she was serving on different committees and foundations. She also had many speaking engagements, and she made frequent trips to New York for special projects at the Rockefeller Institute.

But by 1944, Florence was growing impatient with "all this running around," as she described it. She wanted one big project that would really make use of her talents. So when Governor Vivian asked her to head his subcommittee on health, she was ready.

With her usual thoroughness, she started reading everything she could about public health. She talked to health officials, sewage disposal workers and cattle farmers to gather more information. She put together a committee of the best doctors, lawyers, bankers, civic officials, and dairymen she could find. Together, they developed a set of eight laws that came to be known as the Sabin Health Laws.

By this time, Colorado had a new Governor, Lee Knous. When asked how he would get Florence's health bills and programs passed through the legislature, he supposedly replied, "I'll have the little old lady on my side. There isn't a man . . .

who wants to tangle with her." Early in 1947, all the laws were passed, and the state of Colorado had one of the best public health programs in the nation. Passage of the Sabin Health Laws eventually lowered the death rate in Colorado from one of the highest in the country to one of the lowest.

In 1949, Dr. Sabin went to work as head of Denver's health department. During her three-year term she ended the city's rat problem, improved sewage disposal, set up free x-ray stations throughout the city, and saw to it that only pure milk was sold in Denver's groceries.

Medals, prizes, honors, and awards continued to come — even after her death at the age of eighty-one in 1953. The University of Colorado named a research building after her; and in the city of Denver, a public school bears her name. The state of Colorado finally decided whom to honor in its long-empty spot in Statuary Hall in Washington, D.C.

In a "Cents for Sabin" campaign, the citizens of the state gave their money for a statue of Florence Sabin to be placed in the nation's capital. The only words on this bronze image of the famous doctor are: *Teacher — Scientist — Humanitarian.*

CHIEN SHIUNG WU

Science is not static, but ever-growing and dynamic . . . It is the courage to doubt what has long been established . . . that pushed the wheel of science forward.

Chien Shiung Wu

Dr. Chien Shiung Wu is known among her fellow scientists as the "Queen of Nuclear Physics." Nuclear physics is the study of the nucleus — central part — of the atom, which is made up of protons, neutrons, and other small particles. In 1956, Dr. Wu helped prove that an accepted law of physics was not true. Her experiments changed the way physicists look at nature today.

Chien Shiung Wu was born in Liu Ho, China, on May 29, 1912. Her father was the principal of the local school. He encouraged his daughter's interest in science and mathematics. "There was nothing unusual about women students in China, then as now," Dr. Wu has remarked. "There are more women studying science and engineering in China than in the United States."

Dr. Wu graduated from the National Central University at Nanking in 1936 and then came to the United States to continue her studies. "I wanted to learn everything about the United States," she said, "to absorb the American way of life."

In Berkeley, California, Chien Shiung Wu was a student of Dr. Ernest O. Lawrence when he won the 1939 Nobel Prize in physics. Dr. Lawrence invented the cyclotron, an atom-smashing machine.

For excellent work as a graduate student, Chien Shiung Wu was elected to Phi Beta Kappa, a national honor society. She earned her doctorate degree from the University of California in 1940. Two years later, she married Luke Cha-liou Yuan, a fellow physicist, and the young couple moved from the West coast to the east. Dr. Wu then taught at Smith College and later at Princeton University.

During her teaching and research career, Dr. Wu earned a good reputation as an experimental physicist — a person who tests the ideas or theories of other physicists. Her experience included work with radioactive materials — atoms that give off energy in the form of rays or particles. When two other scientists developed a new idea about the way certain particles behaved, they asked Dr. Wu to test their theory.

Dr. Tsung Dao Lee and Dr. Chen Ning Yang, both Chinese-Americans like Dr. Wu, were questioning the law of parity. This law of physics stated that in nature there is no real difference between right and left — an object and its mirror image behave in the same way.

A way of understanding how this works is to stand in front of a mirror with a corkscrew in one hand and a corked bottle in the other hand. When the corkscrew is turned to the right by the person's right hand, the cork comes out of the bottle. In the mirror, the person appears to be turning the corkscrew to the left, and the cork comes out of the bottle. However, if a person actually did turn the corkscrew to the left, it would not come out of the bottle.

Translating this example to nuclear thinking, the law of parity stated that the cork comes out of the bottle either way the corkscrew is turned. Physicists had believed in the law of parity for thirty years, but it had never been tested.

There was a good reason the parity law had never been examined — it was a very difficult thing to test. Dr. Wu had to find a way to line up a group of radioactive atoms in a row so that their centers were all spinning in the same direction. Then she had to count the number of electrons that flew off the atoms and the direction in which they flew. If the law of parity was right, the same number of electrons would shoot off in opposite directions from the atoms. If more electrons went

Dr. Chien Shiung Wu is pictured in her laboratory. She is standing by the equipment she used to test the law of parity.

one way then another, the law of parity would be proved wrong.

To conduct the experiment, Dr. Wu used special equipment. Radioactive atoms of Cobalt 60 were cooled to extreme temperatures below freezing. A giant magnet lined up the nuclei like atomic tops. A machine called a scintillation counter was used to count the electrons as they shot from the atoms. When Dr. Wu finally conducted the experiment, most of the electrons shot off in one direction. The test results showed that Cobalt 60 behaved like the example of the left-handed corkscrew. The law of parity was disproved.

After the test results were announced to the public in January, 1957, Dr. Lee, Dr. Yang, and Dr. Wu received many honors. That same year, Dr. Lee and Dr. Yang won the Nobel Prize in physics for their work. Among many other honors, Dr. Wu was the first woman to receive an honorary doctor of science degree from Princeton University. She also became the seventh woman member of the National Academy of Sciences, which has been in existence for nearly a century.

In addition to teaching, Dr Wu has continued to do research. Sickle cell anemia — a blood disease which is found primarily in black people — was the focus of her research in the late 1960s. She used the tools of basic nuclear physics to find proof that certain blood cells change shape and plug up tiny blood vessels in the human body. When this happens, blood does not circulate throughout the body as it should.

In recent years, Dr. Wu has returned to the study of radioactive atoms. The famous woman physicist has continued to receive honors. At the White House, in 1976, President Ford presented her with the National Medal of Science, the highest science award in the United States. And, in 1978, she was named the first winner of the $100,000 Wolf Prize in physics. Wanting to share the benefits of her achievements, Dr. Wu started a scholarship fund for Chinese-American science students.

Dr. Wu is proud of being a woman in science. "I wish there were more opportunities for women in science," she has said. "Never before have so few contributed so much."

She is quick to point to the achievements of other women in her profession. Marie Curie was the only person to win two Nobel Prizes in science — one in physics and one in chemistry. Irene Joliet-Curie, along with her husband, won a Nobel Prize in chemistry. Maria Goeppert-Mayer was the first American woman, and the only woman besides Marie Curie, to win a Nobel Prize in physics.

Not long after Dr. Wu completed the experiment which overthrew the law of parity, she told a group of young science students, "Science is not static but ever-growing and dynamic. . . It is the courage to doubt what has long been established. . . that pushed the wheel of science forward."

BIBLIOGRAPHY

Bluemel, Elinor. *Florence Sabin: Colorado Woman of the Century.* Boulder, Colo.: University of Colorado Press, 1959.

Brooks, Paul. *The House of Life: Rachel Carson at Work* Boston: Houghton Mifflin, 1972.

Hamilton, Alice. *Exploring the Dangerous Trades: The Autobiography of Alice Hamilton, M.D.* Boston: Little, Brown & Co., Atlantic Monthly Press, 1943.

McDowell, Barbara, ed., and Umlauf, Hana, ed. *The Good Housekeeping Woman's Almanac.* New York: Newspaper Enterprise Association, 1977.

Mead, Margaret. *Blackberry Winter: My Earlier Years.* New York: William Morrow & Co., 1972.

Phelan, Mary K. *Probing the Unknown.* New York: Dell Publishing, 1976.

Yost, Edna. *American Women of Science.* Philadelphia: J.B. Lippincott, 1955.

Yost, Edna. *Women of Modern Science.* New York: Dodd, Mead & Co., 1959.